I0814810

A Gorilla's World
Katie Gillespie
EYEDISCOVER

Go to **www.eyediscover.com** and enter this book's unique code.

BOOK CODE

T996857

EYEDISCOVER brings you optic readalongs that support active learning.

Published by AV² by Weigl
350 5th Avenue, 59th Floor New York, NY 10118
Website: www.eyediscover.com

Library of Congress Control Number: 2017930714

ISBN 978-1-4896-5659-9 (hardcover)

Printed in the United States of America
in Brainerd, Minnesota
1 2 3 4 5 6 7 8 9 0 21 20 19 18 17

022017
020317

Editor: Katie Gillespie
Designer: Mandy Christiansen

Weigl acknowledges Getty Images, iStock, and Alamy as the primary image suppliers for this title.

EYEDISCOVER provides enriched content, optimized for tablet use, that supplements and complements this book. EYEDISCOVER books strive to create inspired learning and engage young minds in a total learning experience.

Watch
Video content brings each page to life.

Browse
Thumbnails make navigation simple.

Read
Follow along with text on the screen.

Listen
Hear each page read aloud.

Your EYEDISCOVER Optic Readalongs come alive with...

Audio
Listen to the entire book read aloud.

Video
High resolution videos turn each spread into an optic readalong.

OPTIMIZED FOR

- ✓ TABLETS
- ✓ WHITEBOARDS
- ✓ COMPUTERS
- ✓ AND MUCH MORE!

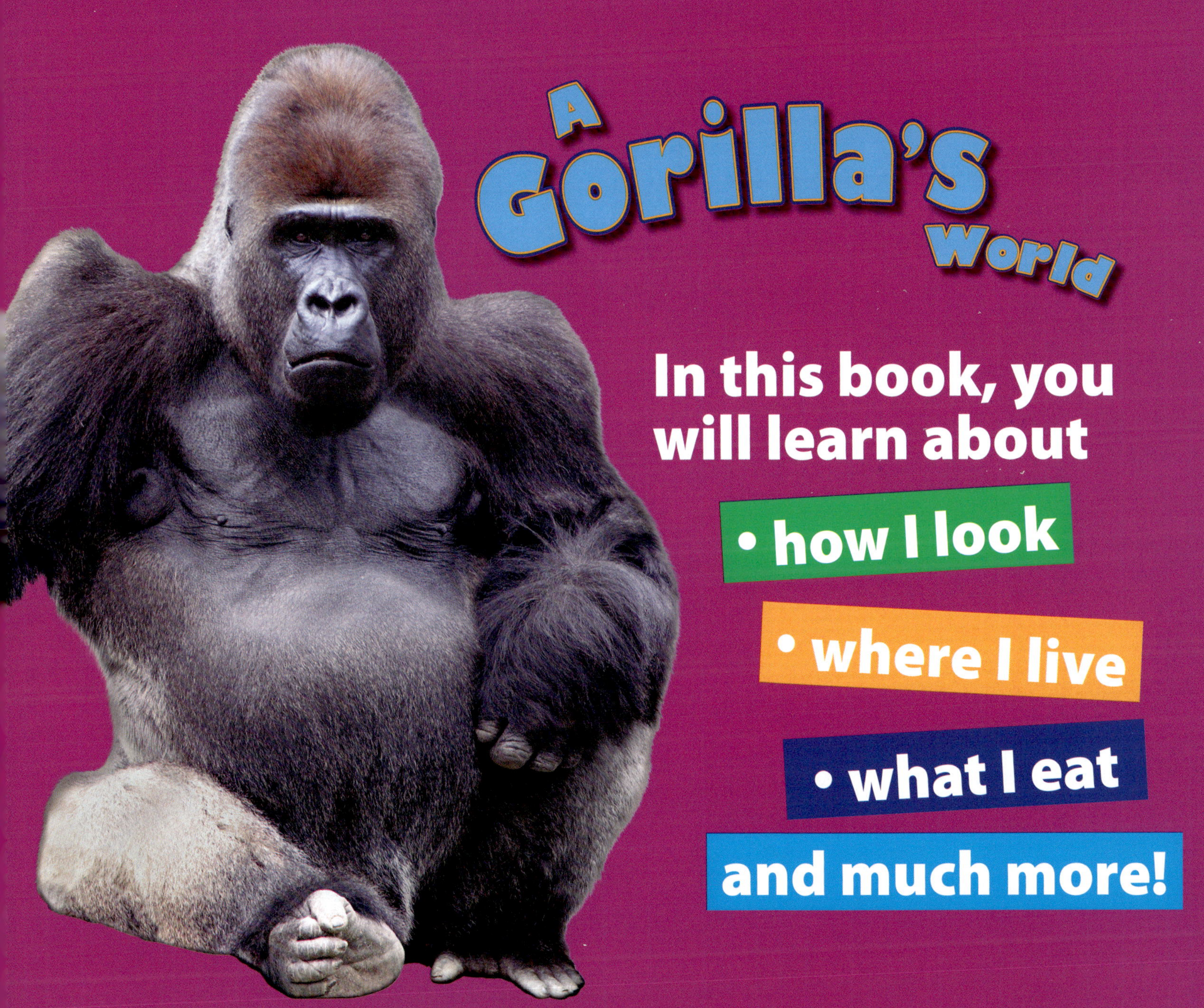

A Gorilla's World

In this book, you will learn about

- **how I look**
- **where I live**
- **what I eat**

and much more!

I am a gorilla.

I am a large animal with dark hair and long arms. I am the biggest of all the apes.

I live in the forests of Africa.

I rode on my mother's back when I was young. I learned to climb trees when I grew older.

I can stand on two feet, but usually walk on all fours.

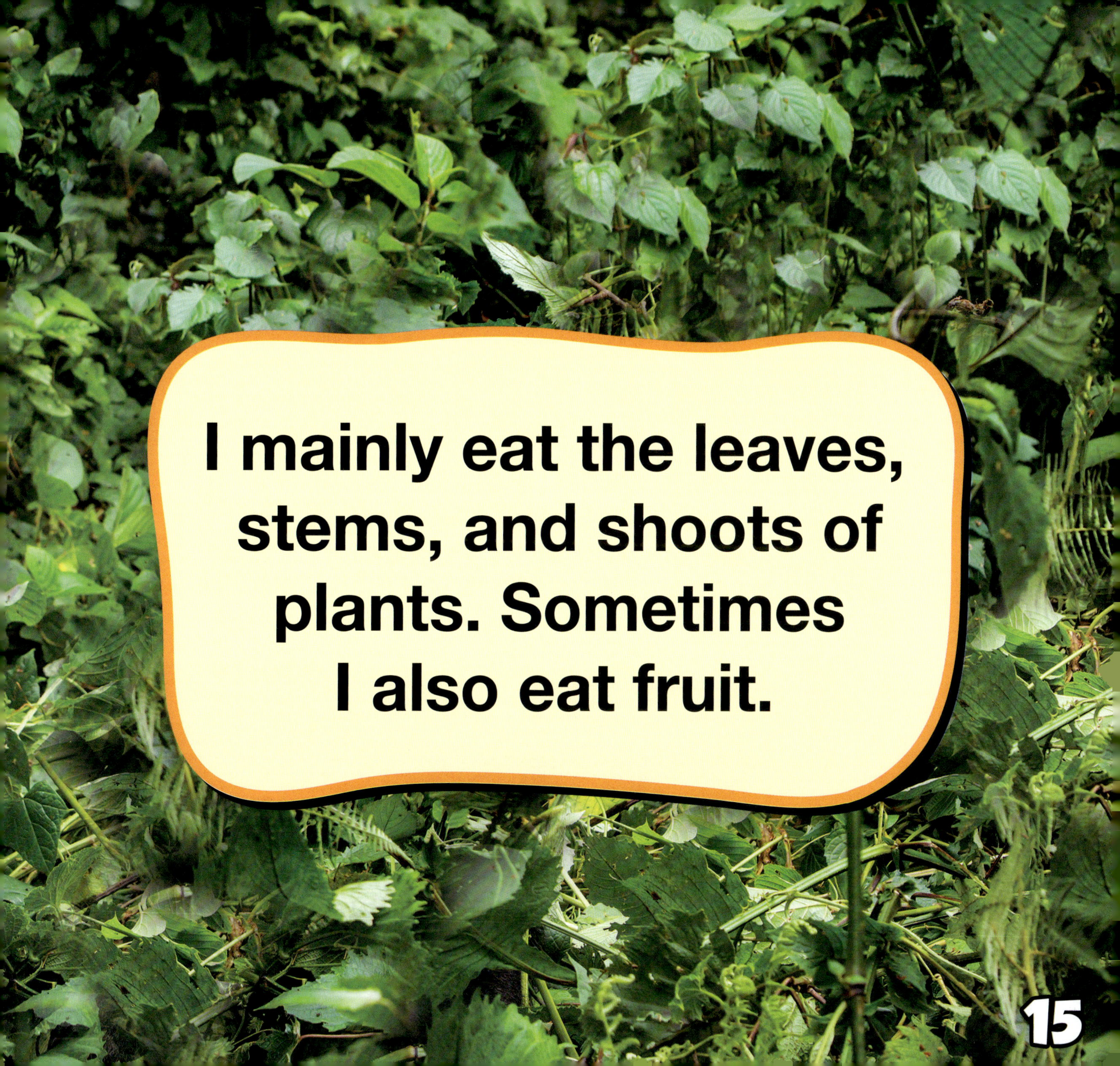
I mainly eat the leaves, stems, and shoots of plants. Sometimes I also eat fruit.

My family and I live together. Our group is called a troop.

I talk to my troop by slapping my chest.

I need a home near plants to stay happy and healthy.

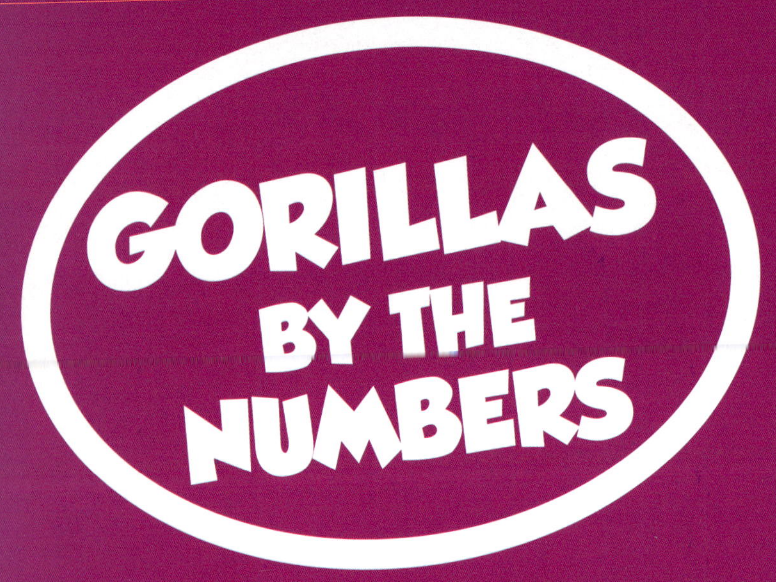

Gorillas eat more than **100 different** kinds of plants.

A gorilla **eats** for about **seven hours** each day.

Baby gorillas drink their **mother's milk** for their first **2.5 years.**

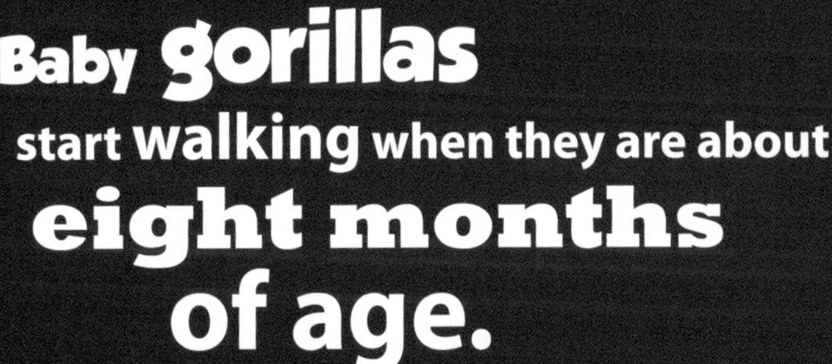

Baby gorillas start **walking** when they are about **eight months** of age.

There are **only** about **100,000** gorillas left **in nature.**

KEY WORDS

Research has shown that as much as 65 percent of all written material published in English is made up of 300 words. These 300 words cannot be taught using pictures or learned by sounding them out. They must be recognized by sight. This book contains 44 common sight words to help young readers improve their reading fluency and comprehension. This book also teaches young readers several important content words, such as proper nouns. These words are paired with pictures to aid in learning and improve understanding.

Page	Sight Words First Appearance
4	a, am, I
7	all, and, animal, large, long, of, the, with
8	in, live
11	back, grew, mother, my, on, to, trees, was, when, young
12	but, can, feet, fours, two, walk
15	also, eat, leaves, plants, sometimes
16	family, group, is, our, together
19	by, talk
20	home, near, need

Page	Content Words First Appearance
4	gorilla
7	apes, arms, hair
8	Africa, forests
15	fruit, shoots, stems
16	troop
19	chest

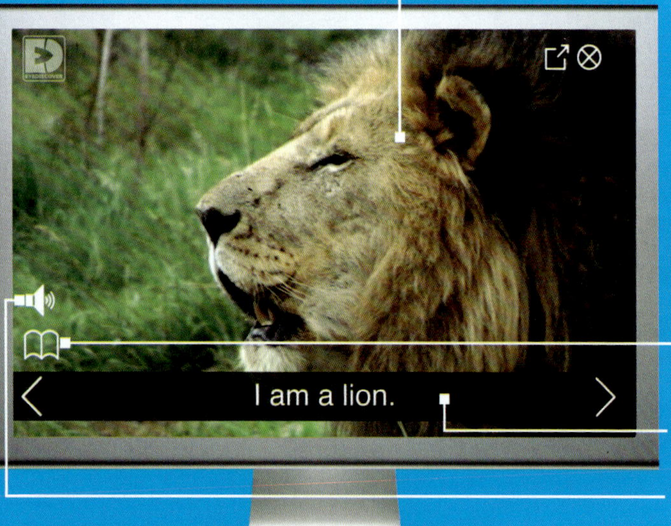

Watch
Video content brings each page to life.

Browse
Thumbnails make navigation simple.

Read
Follow along with text on the screen.

Listen
Hear each page read aloud.

Go to www.eyediscover.com and enter this book's unique code.

BOOK CODE

T996857